W0007853

AUSTRALIAN VERSE

A Sunburnt Country

Duncan Cooper, 1813 or 14–1904, *On the plains near Challicum*, watercolour 17.1 x 24.1 cm, *The Challicum Sketch Book*. National Library of Australia.

AUSTRALIAN VERSE

A Sunburnt Country

ILLUSTRATED WITH AUSTRALIAN LANDSCAPE PAINTINGS

Selected by Margaret Olds

MURRAY DAVID PUBLISHING

Published by
Murray David Publishing Pty Ltd
33a Carnarvon Drive, Frenchs Forest, NSW, 2086

Designed by Murray Child and Emma Seymour
This collection of poems and paintings
© Murray David Publishing Pty Ltd, 1998
© Design, Murray David Publishing Pty Ltd, 1998
Digital colour separation and film by Typescan, Adelaide
Printed in Indonesia

ISBN 1 876411 57 0 (set).
ISBN 1 876411 58 9 (Banjo Paterson).
ISBN 1 876411 59 7 (Henry lawson).
ISBN 1 876411 60 0 (Australian Verse Collection).

Contents

Introduction

From the early days of colonial settlement Australia has had a strong verse tradition, inherited from the English, the Irish and the Scots. During the nineteenth century we made that tradition firmly our own, as nameless bush poets flourished, and poems, songs and stories passed from traveller to traveller among bushmen, drovers, shearers and swaggies, around campfires all over Australia.

Simple rhymes and galloping rhythms made the poems memorable, but even so, slightly different versions of many of the early poems and songs have been collected in different areas by folklorists. Many of the early ballads display laconic humour in the face of adversity (supposedly a characteristic of Australian bushmen—or even of all Australians). "Holy Dan" is a good example of this. Dan, eschewing bad language, prays not to lose his bullocks in a drought, but as they die one by one, his language deteriorates and he tells God he might as well take the b—— lot. The twist of fate (or act of God) is the final thunderstorm in which Dan is drowned.

Poets like Henry Kendall, Adam Lindsay Gordon and Will Ogilvie follow in the bush ballad tradition. And of course there is the most famous ballad of them all, "The Man from Snowy River", by A. B. (the "Banjo") Paterson, which has been known and loved by generations of Australians.

Many of the early poems have the bush as a motivating force and show humans in conflict with it. As the land was gradually tamed and settlement spread, poets of the late nineteenth and early twentieth centuries such as John Shaw Neilson and Christopher Brennan turned to a more lyrical style, celebrating the bush.

This tradition continued and can be seen flowering in Dorothea Mackellar's famous poem, "My Country". Published in 1908, "My Country" was learned by generations of school children. Many years later, some of us find we can still recite verse after verse!

Today, when Australia is a highly urbanised country with most of the population living around the coast, Australians remember their bush heritage and continue to respond to the poems and songs of an earlier time. Most of us can say with Dorothea Mackellar, "The wide brown land for me!"

MARGARET OLDS

My Country

DOROTHEA MACKELLAR

The love of field and coppice
Of green and shaded lanes,
Of ordered woods and gardens
Is running in your veins.
Strong love of grey-blue distance,
Brown streams and soft, dim skies—
I know, but cannot share it,
My love is otherwise.

I love a sunburnt country,
A land of sweeping plains,
Of rugged mountain ranges,
Of droughts and flooding rains.
I love her far horizons,
I love her jewel-sea,
Her beauty and her terror—
The wide brown land for me!

The stark white ring-barked forests,
All tragic to the moon,
The sapphire-misted mountains,
The hot gold hush of noon,
Green tangle of the brushes
Where lithe lianas coil,
And orchids deck the tree-tops,
And ferns the warm dark soil.

Core of my heart, my country!
Her pitiless blue sky,
When, sick at heart, around us

Elioth Gruner, Australia, 1882–1939, *The Valley Of The Tweed,* 1921, oil on canvas 142.2 x 172.7 cm.
Commissioned by the Trustees 1919. Received 1921. Art Gallery of New South Wales.

We see the cattle die—
But then the grey clouds gather,
And we can bless again
The drumming of an army,
The steady soaking rain.

Core of my heart, my country!
Land of the rainbow gold,
For flood and fire and famine
She pays us back threefold.

Over the thirsty paddocks,
Watch, after many days,
The filmy veil of greenness
That thickens as we gaze...

An opal-hearted country,
A wilful, lavish land—
All you who have not loved her,
You will not understand—
Though Earth holds many splendours,
Wherever I may die,
I know to what brown country
My homing thoughts will fly.

Song of the Cattle Hunters

HENRY KENDALL

While the morning light beams on the fern-matted streams,
   And the water-pools flash in its glow,
Down the ridges we fly, with a loud ringing cry—
   Down the ridges and gullies we go!
And the cattle we hunt, they are racing in front,
   With a roar like the thunder of waves;
As the beat and the beat of our swift horses' feet
   Start the echoes away from their caves!
              As the beat and the beat
              Of our swift horses' feet
         Start the echoes away from their caves!

Like a wintery shore that the waters ride o'er,
   All the lowlands are filling with sound;
For swiftly we gain where the herds on the plain,
   Like a tempest, are tearing the ground!
And we'll follow them hard to the rails of the yard,
   Over gulches and mountain-tops grey,
Where the beat and the beat of our swift horses' feet
   Will die with the echoes away!
              Where the beat and the beat
              Of our swift horses' feet
         Will die with the echoes away!

Duncan Cooper, 1813 or 14–1904, *Challicum, 1844,* watercolour 17.3 x 26.4 cm, *The Challicum Sketch Book.* National Library of Australia.

The Sick Stockrider

ADAM LINDSAY GORDON

Hold hard, Ned! Lift me down once more, and lay me in the
    shade.
Old man, you've had your work cut out to guide
Both horses, and to hold me in the saddle when I sway'd,
All through the hot, slow, sleepy, silent ride.

The dawn at "Moorabinda" was a mist rack dull and dense,
The sunrise was a sullen, sluggish lamp;
I was dozing in the gateway at Arbuthnot's bound'ry fence,
I was dreaming on the limestone cattle camp.

We crossed the creek at Carricksford, and sharply through the
    haze,
And suddenly, the sun shot flaming forth;
To the southward lay "Katawa", with the sandpeaks all ablaze,
And the flush'd fields of Glen Lomond lay to north.

Now westward winds the bridle path that leads to Lindisfarm,
And yonder looms the double-headed Bluff;
From the far side of the first hill, when the skies are clear and
    calm,
You can see Sylvester's woolshed fair enough.

Five miles we used to call it from our homestead to the place
Where the big tree spans the roadway like an arch;
'Twas here we ran the dingo down that gave us such a chase
Eight years ago—or was it nine?—last March.

'Twas merry in the glowing morn, among the gleaming
    grass,
To wander as we've wandered many a mile,

And blow the cool tobacco cloud, and watch the white wreaths
     pass,
Sitting loosely in the saddle all the while.

'Twas merry 'mid the blackwoods, when we spied the station
     roofs,
To wheel the wild scrub cattle at the yard,
With a running fire of stockwhips and fiery run of hoofs;
Oh! the hardest day was never then too hard!

Aye! we had a glorious gallop after "Starlight" and his gang,
When they bolted from Sylvester's on the flat;

John Longstaff, *Breaking the News*, 1887. Acquired with funds from the Haclett Bequest 1933.
Art Gallery of Western Australia.

15

How the sun-dried reed-beds crackled, how the flint-strewn
    ranges rang
To the strokes of "Mountaineer" and "Acrobat"!

Hard behind them in the timber, harder still across the heath,
Close beside them through the tea-tree scrub we dashed;
And the golden-tinted fern leaves, how they rustled
    underneath!
And the honeysuckle osiers, how they crash'd!

We led the hunt throughout, Ned, on the chestnut and the
    grey,
And the troopers were three hundred yards behind,
While we emptied our six-shooters on the bushrangers at bay,
In the creek with stunted box-tree for a blind!

There you grappled with the leader, man to man and horse
    to horse,
And you roll'd together when the chestnut rear'd;
He blazed away and missed you in that shallow watercourse—
A narrow shave—his powder singed your beard!

In these hours when life is ebbing, how those days when life
    was young
Come back to us; how clearly I recall
Even the yarns Jack Hall invented, and the songs Jem Roper
    sung;
And where are now Jem Roper and Jack Hall?

Aye! nearly all our comrades of the old colonial school,
Our ancient boon companions, Ned, are gone;
Hard livers for the most part, somewhat reckless as rule,
It seems that you and I are left alone.

There was Hughes, who got in trouble through that business
  with the cards,
It matters little what became of him;
But a steer ripp'd up MacPherson in the Cooraminta yards,
And Sullivan was drown'd at Sink-or-swim.

And Mostyn—poor Frank Mostyn—died at last a fearful wreck,
In "the horrors", at the Upper Wandinong;
And Carisbrooke, the rider, at the Horsefall broke his neck—
Faith! the wonder was, he saved his neck so long!

Ah! those days and nights we squandered at the Logans' in the
  glen—
The Logans, man and wife, have long been dead.
Elsie's tallest girl seems taller than your little Elsie then;
And Ethel is a woman grown and wed.

I've had my share of pastime, and I've done my share of toil,
And life is short—the longest life a span;
I care not now to tarry for the corn or for the oil,
Or for the wine that maketh glad the heart of man.

For good undone and gifts misspent and resolutions vain,
'Tis somewhat late to trouble. This I know—
I should live the same life over, if I had to live again;
And the chances are I go where most men go.

The deep blue skies wax dusky, and the tall green trees grow
  dim,
The sward beneath me seems to heave and fall;
And sickly, smoky shadows through the sleepy sunlight swim,
And on the very sun's face weave their pall.

Let me slumber in the hollow where the wattle blossoms wave,
With never stone or rail to fence my bed;
Should the sturdy station children pull the bush flowers on my
　　grave,
I may chance to hear them romping overhead.

I don't suppose I shall, though, for I feel like sleeping sound.
That sleep they say is doubtful. True; but yet
At least it makes no difference to the dead man underground
What the living men remember or forget.

Enigmas that perplex us in the world's unequal strife,
The future may ignore or may reveal.
YET SOME, AS WEAK AS WATER, NED! TO MAKE THE BEST OF LIFE,
HAVE BEEN, TO FACE THE WORST, AS TRUE AS STEEL.

Northward to the Sheds

WILL H. OGILVIE

There's a whisper from the regions out beyond the Barwon
　　banks;
There's a gathering of the legions and a forming of the ranks;
There's a murmur coming nearer with the signs that never
　　fail,
And it's time for every shearer to be out upon the trail.
They must leave their goals behind them and their empty
　　glasses, too,
For there's plenty left to mind them when they cross the dry
　　Barcoo;
There'll be kissing, there'll be sorrow such as only sweethearts
　　know,
But before the noon tomorrow they'll be singing as they go—

Hans Heysen, Australia, 1877–1968, *Droving into the light*, 1921. Presented by W. H. Vincent 1922. Art Gallery of Western Australia. Reproduced with the kind permission of Mr C. Heysen.

> *For the Western creeks are calling,*
> *And the idle days are done,*
> *With the snowy fleeces falling*
> *And the Queensland sheds begun!*

There is shortening of the bridle, there is tightening of the
  girth,
There is fondling of the idol that they love the best on earth;
Northward from the Lachlan River and the sun-dried
  Castlereagh,
Outward to the Never-Never ride the ringers on their way.

From the green bends of the Murray they have run their
    horses in,
For there's haste and there is hurry when the Queensland
    sheds begin;
On the Bogan they are bridling, they are saddling on the
    Bland,
There is plunging and there's sidling—for the colts don't
    understand

> *That the Western creeks are calling,*
> *And the idle days are done,*
> *With the snowy fleeces falling*
> *And the Queensland sheds begun!*

They will camp below the station, they'll be cutting peg and
    pole,
Rearing tents for occupation, till the calling of the roll;
And it's time the nags were driven, and it's time to strap the
    pack,
For there's never licence given to the laggards on the track.
Hark the music of the battle! it is time to bare our swords:
Do you hear the rush and rattle as they tramp along the
    boards?
They past the pen-doors picking light-wooled weaners one by
    one;
I can hear the shear-blades clicking, and I know the fight's
    begun!

Holy Dan

ANON.

It was in the Queensland drought,
  And over hill and dell,
No grass—the water far apart,
  All dry and hot as hell.
The wretched bullock teams drew up
  Beside a water-hole—
They'd struggled on through dust and drought,
  For days to reach this goal.

And though the water rendered forth,
  A rank, unholy stench,
The bullocks and the bullockies
  Drank deep, their thirst to quench.

Two of the drivers cursed and swore,
  As only drivers can.
The other one, named Daniel,
  Best known as Holy Dan,
Admonished them and said it was
  The Lord's all-wise decree,
And if they'd only watch and wait,
  A change they'd quickly see.

"Twas strange that of Dan's bullocks,
  Not one had gone aloft,
But this, he said, was due to prayer
  And supplication oft.
At last, one died but Dan was calm,
  He hardly seemed to care.
He knelt beside the bullock's corpse,
  And offered up a prayer.

"One bullock, Thou hast taken, Lord,
    And so it seemeth best.
Thy will be done, but see my need,
    And spare to me the rest!"

A month went by. Dan's bullocks now
    Were dying every day,
But still on each occasion would
    The faithful fellow pray,
"Another Thou hast taken, Lord,
    And so it seemeth best.
Thy will be done, but see my need,
    And spare to me the rest!"

And still they camped beside the hole,
    And still it never rained,
And still Dan's bullocks died and died,
    Till only one remained.
Then Dan broke down—good, Holy Dan—
    The man who never swore.
He knelt beside the latest corpse,
    And here's the prayer he prore.

"That's nineteen Thou hast taken, Lord,
    And now You'll plainly see,
You'd better take the bloody lot,
    One's no damn good to me."
The other riders laughed so much
    They shook the sky around;
The lightning flashed, the thunder roared,
    And Holy Dan was drowned.

The Man from Snowy River

A. B. "BANJO" PATERSON

There was movement at the station, for the word had passed
    around
That the colt from old Regret had got away,
And had joined the wild bush horses—he was worth a thou-
    sand pound,
So all the cracks had gathered to the fray.
All the tried and noted riders from the stations near and far
Had mustered at the homestead overnight,
For the bushmen love hard riding where the wild bush horses
    are,
And the stock-horse snuffs the battle with delight.

There was Harrison, who made his pile when Pardon won the
    cup,
The old man with his hair as white as snow;
But few could ride beside him when his blood was fairly up—
He would go wherever horse and man could go.
And Clancy of the Overflow came down to lend a hand,
No better horseman ever held the reins;
For never horse could throw him while the saddle girths would
    stand,
He learnt to ride while droving on the plains.

And one was there, a stripling on a small and weedy beast,
He was something like a racehorse undersized,
With a touch of Timor pony—three parts thoroughbred at
    least—
And such as are by mountain horsemen prized.
He was hard and tough and wiry—just the sort that won't say
    die—
There was courage in his quick impatient tread;

And he bore the badge of gameness in his bright and fiery
    eye,
And the proud and lofty carriage of his head.

But so slight and weedy, one would doubt his power to stay,
And the old man said, "That horse will never do
For a long and tiring gallop—lad, you'd better stop away,
Those hills are far too rough for such as you."
So he waited sad and wistful—only Clancy stood his friend—
"I think we ought to let him come," he said;

Eugene von Guerard,
Australia, 1811–1901,
*North-east view from
the northern top of
Mount Kosciusko,*
1863, oil on canvas
66.5 x 116.8 cm.
National Gallery of
Australia, Canberra.

"I warrant he'll be with us when he's wanted at the end,
For both his horse and he are mountain bred.

"He hails from Snowy River, up by Kosciusko's side,
Where the hills are twice as steep and twice as rough,
Where a horse's hoofs strike firelight from the flint stones
     every stride,
The man that holds his own is good enough.
And the Snowy River riders on the mountains make their
     home,

Where the river runs those giant hills between;
I have seen full many horsemen since I first commenced to
    roam,
But nowhere yet such horsemen have I seen."

So he went—they found the horses by the big mimosa
    clump—
They raced away towards the mountain's brow,
And the old man gave his orders, "Boys, go at them from the
    jump,
No use to try for fancy riding now.
And, Clancy, you must wheel them, try and wheel them to the
    right.
Ride boldly, lad, and never fear the spills,
For never yet was rider that could keep the mob in sight,
If once they gain the shelter of those hills."

So Clancy rode to wheel them—he was racing on the wing
Where the best and boldest riders take their place,
And he raced his stockhorse past them, and he made the
    ranges ring
With stockwhip, as he met them face to face.
Then they halted for a moment, while he swung the dreaded
    lash,
But they saw their well-loved mountain full in view,
And they charged beneath the stockwhip with a sharp and sud-
    den dash,
And off into the mountain scrub they flew.

Then fast the horsemen followed, where the gorges deep and
    black
Resounded to the thunder of their tread,
And the stockwhips woke the echoes, and they fiercely
    answered back

From cliffs and crags that beetled overhead.
And upward, ever upward, the wild horses held their sway,
Where mountain ash and kurrajong grew wide;
And the old man muttered fiercely, "We may bid the mob
    good day,
No man can hold them down the other side."

When they reached the mountain's summit, even Clancy took
    a pull,
It well might make the boldest hold their breath,
The wild hop scrub grew thickly, and the hidden ground was
    full
Of wombat holes, and any slip was death.
But the man from Snowy River let the pony have his head,
And he swung his stockwhip round and gave a cheer,
And he raced him down the mountain like a torrent down its
    bed,
While the others stood and watched in very fear.

He sent the flint stones flying, but the pony kept his feet,
He cleared the fallen timbers in his stride,
And the man from Snowy River never shifted in his seat—
It was grand to see that mountain horseman ride.
Through the stringybarks and saplings, on the rough and
    broken ground,
Down the hillside at a racing pace he went;
And he never drew the bridle till he landed safe and sound,
At the bottom of that terrible descent.

He was right among the horses as they climbed the further hill
And the watchers on the mountain standing mute,
Saw him ply the stockwhip fiercely, he was right among them
    still,
As he raced across the clearing in pursuit.

Then they lost him for a moment, where two mountain gullies met
In the ranges, but a final glimpse reveals
On a dim and distant hillside the wild horses racing yet,
With the man from Snowy River at their heels.

And he ran them single-handed till their sides were white with foam.
He followed like a bloodhound in their track,
Till they halted cowed and beaten, then he turned their heads for home,
And alone and unassisted brought them back.
But his hardy mountain pony he could scarcely raise a trot,
He was blood from hip to shoulder from the spur;
But his pluck was still undaunted, and his courage fiery hot,
For never yet was mountain horse a cur.

And down by Kosciusko, where the pine-clad ridges raise
Their torn and rugged battlements on high,
Where the air is clear as crystal, and the white stars fairly blaze
At midnight in the cold and frosty sky,
And where around The Overflow the reed beds sweep and sway
To the breezes, and the rolling plains are wide,
The man from Snowy River is a household word today,
And the stockmen tell the story of his ride.

Catching the Coach

ALFRED T. CHANDLER

At Kangaroo Gully in 'Fifty-two
The rush and the scramble was reckless and rough;
"Three ounces a dish and the lead running true!"
Was whispered around concerning the stuff.

Next morning a thousand of fellows or more
Appeared for invasion along the brown rise,
Some Yankees, and Cockneys and Cantabs of yore
And B.A.s from Oxford in blue-shirt disguise.

And two mornings later the Nugget saloon,
With billiards and skittles, was glaring with signs,
A blind fiddler, Jim, worried out a weak tune,
Beguiling the boys and collecting the fines.

Then tents started up like the freaks of a dream
While heaps of white pipeclay dotted the slope,
To "Dern her—a duffer!" or "Creme de la creme!"
That settled the verdict of languishing hope.

And bustle and jollity rang through the trees
In strange combination of humankind traits;
With feverish searchings and gay levities
The fires of excitement were fully ablaze.

Well, three mornings after, the stringybark gums
All rustled their leaves with further surprise;
They'd seen old stagers and limey new-chums,
But here were galoots in peculiar guise:

With nondescript uniform, booted and spurred,
A fierce-looking strap on the underneath lip,
An ominous shooter, a dangling sword,
A grim leather pouch above the right hip!

And maybe a dozen came cantering so,
All clanking and jaunty—authority vain—
When down through the gully rang out the word "Joe",
And "Joe" was sent on with a sneering refrain.

There was hunting for "rights", and producing the same,
Or passing them on to a paperless mate,
Or hiding in bushes or down in the claim—
Such various expedients to baffle the State.

Then "Who put him on?"—"'Twig his illigant seat!'"
"Cuss me, but it's purty!"—"The thing on the horse!"
"His first dacent clothes!"—"What surprise for his feet!"
Such volleys as these were soon fired at the Force.

But duty was duty. Just then through the scrub
A digger made off—he a culprit no doubt!
"Dismount you then, Wilson!" roared Sergeant Hubbub;
"Quick! follow the rascal and ferret him out."

The sapling cadet, with budding moustache,
Then sprang to the ground in dauntless pursuit
And, filled up with zeal and a soldier-like dash,
He felt a true hero of saddle and boot.

The gully quick echoed with taunts that were real,
Keen chaff of defiance allied to revolt,
Such sharp wordy weapons as might have been steel
From skirmishers laughing on hillock and holt.

Away went the fugitive, spurred on by haste,
Escaping the undergrowth, leaping the logs,
Yet ne'er looking back—did he know he was chased?
Said Wilson, "He's one of the worst of the dogs!

"Some greater misdeed must have blackened his hand;
I'll have him—promotion! Stop there, or I'll shoot!"
The other ahead didn't hear the command
But sprang on unheeding o'er dry branch and root.

The chase settled down to a heavy set-to;
They ran o'er the hill and across the clear flat;
And Wilson was chuckling—the villain he knew
Was making a bee-line for jail—Ballarat!

"I'll follow the rogue safely into the trap—
Confound him, he's speedy: I can't run him down;
But there, quite unconscious of any mishap,
I'll fix him up neatly in gay Canvas Town!"

Then over a creek where a line of sage-gums
All flourishing grew, then away to the right;
There loud breathings mingled with strange forest hums,
And wallabies scampered with terror and fright.

And cockatoos screeched from the loftiest trees,
The minahs and magpies all fluttered and flew,
The drowsy old possums were roused from their ease,
The locusts and lizards quick stepped out of view.

But on went the pair, never noticing this,
For both had a serious business in hand.
With one there were feelings that prophesied bliss,
The other saw capture and glory so grand.

O'er hillside and creek, beyond hollow and spur,
Though brief strips of woodland, they hurried on still;
The trooper lost ground, but he wasn't a cur;
Besides, they were nearing on Bakery Hill.

Then suddenly broke on each sweltering sight
The thousand of tents in the city of gold;
And straight to the thick of them ran with delight
The chased and the chaser—what luck for the bold!

The coach was just starting for Melbourne that day
As Wilson rushed eagerly on to his man.
"I'll put you with care where you won't be so gay,"
The trooper in triumph already began.

"You've led me a dance in a lively hour's sun;
Now trip out your licence, or waltz off to jail!
What! got one? Oh, ho! Why the —— did you run?"
"To post this here letter for Nell by the mail."

A Flight of Wild Ducks

CHARLES HARPUR

Far up the River—hark! 'tis the loud shock
Deadened by distance, of some Fowler's gun:
And as into the stillness of the scene
It wastes now with a dull vibratory boom,
Look where, fast widening up at either end
Out of the sinuous valley of the waters,
And o'er the intervenient forest,—up
Against the open heaven, a long dark *line*
Comes hitherward stretching—a vast Flight of Ducks!
Following the winding of the vale, and still
Enlarging lengthwise, and in places too
Oft breaking into solitary dots,
How swiftly onwards comes it—till at length,
The River, reaching through a group of hills,
Off leads it,—out of sight. But not for long:
For, wheeling ever with the water's course,
Here into sudden view it comes again
Sweeping and swarming round the nearest point!
And first now, a swift airy rush is heard
Approaching momently;—then all at once
There passes a keen-cutting, gusty tumult
Of strenuous pinions, with a streaming mass
Of instantaneous skiey streaks; each streak
Evolving with a lateral flirt, and thence
Entangling as it were,—so rapidly
A thousand wings outpointingly dispread
In passing tiers, seem, looked at from beneath,
With rushing intermixtures to involve
Each other as they beat. Thus seen o'erhead
Even while we speak—ere we have spoken,—lo!

The living cloud is onward many a rood,
Tracking as 'twere in the smooth stream below
The multifarious shadow of itself.
Far coming—present—and far gone at once!
The senses vainly struggle to retain
The impression of an Image (as the same)
So swift and manifold: For now again
A long dark *line* upon the utmost verge
Of the horizon, steeping still, it sinks
At length into the landscape; where yet seen
Though dimly, with a wide and scattering sweep
It fetches eastward, and in column so
Dapples along the steep face of the ridge

G. Devereux, *Murray River*, 1877, oil on academy board, 22.6 x 30.3 cm. National Library of
Australia.

There banking the turned River. Now it drops
Below the fringing oaks—but to arise
Once more, with a quick circling gleam, as touched
By the slant sunshine, and then disappear
As instantaneously,—there settling down
Upon the reedy bosom of the water.

Where the Dead Men Lie

BARCROFT BOAKE

Out on the wastes of the Never Never—
    That's where the dead men lie!
There where the heat-waves dance for ever—
    That's where the dead men lie!
That's where the Earth's loved sons are keeping
Endless tryst: not the west wind sweeping
Feverish pinions can wake their sleeping—
    Out where the dead men lie!

Where brown Summer and Death have mated—
    That's where the dead men lie!
Loving with fiery lust unsated—
    That's where the dead men lie!
Out where the grinning skulls bleach whitely
    Under the saltbush sparkling brightly;
Out where the wild dogs chorus nightly—
    That's where the dead men lie!

Deep in the yellow, flowing river—
    That's where the dead men lie!
Under the banks where the shadows quiver—
    That's where the dead men lie!
Where the platypus twists and doubles,
Leaving a train of tiny bubbles;

Rid at last of their earthly troubles—
    That's where the dead men lie!

East and backward pale faces turning—
    That's how the dead men lie!
Gaunt arms stretched with a voiceless yearning—
    That's how the dead men lie!
Oft in the fragrant hush of nooning
Hearing again their mother's crooning,
Wrapt for aye in a dreamful swooning—
    That's how the dead men lie!

Only the hand of Night can free them—
    That's when the dead men fly!

Duncan Cooper, 1813 or 14–1904, *On the plains near Challicum*, watercolour 17.1 x 24.1 cm,
The Challicum Sketch Book. National Library of Australia.

36

Only the frightened cattle see them—
    See the dead men go by!
Cloven hoofs beating out one measure,
Bidding the stockmen know no leisure—
That's when the dead men take their pleasure!
    That's when the dead men fly!

Ask, too, the never-sleeping drover:
    He sees the dead pass by;
Hearing them call to their friends—the plover,
    Hearing the dead men cry;
Seeing their faces stealing, stealing,
Hearing their laughter, pealing pealing,
Watching their grey forms wheeling, wheeling
    Round where the cattle lie!

Strangled by thirst and fierce privation—
    That's how the dead men die!
Out on Moneygrub's farthest station—
    That's how the dead men die!
Hard-faced greybeards, youngsters callow;
Some mounds cared for, some left fallow;
Some deep down, yet others shallow;
    Some having but the sky.

Moneygrub, as he sips his claret,
    Looks with complacent eye
Down at his watch-chain, eighteen carat—
    There, in his club, hard by:
Recks not that every link is stamped with
Names of the men whose limbs are cramped with
Too long lying in grave-mould, cramped with
    Death where the dead men lie.

She is the Night

CHRISTOPHER BRENNAN

She is the night: all horror is of her
heap'd, shapeless, on the unclaim'd chaotic marsh
or huddled on the looming sepulchre
where the incult and scanty herb is harsh.

She is the night: all terror is of her
when the distemper'd dark begins to boil
with wavering face of larve and oily blur
of pallor on her suffocating coil.

David Davies, Australia, 1863–1939, *Moonrise,* oil on canvas 50 x 60 cm. Elder Bequest Fund 1947. Art Gallery of South Australia.

Or majesty is hers, when marble gloom
supports her, calm, with glittering signs severe
and grandeur of metallic roof of doom,
far in the windows of our broken sphere.

Or she can be all pale, under no moon
or star, with veiling of the glamour cloud,
all pale, as were the fainting secret soon
to be exhaled, bride-robed in clinging shroud.

For she is night, and knows each wooing mood:
and her warm breasts are near in the charm'd air
of summer eve, and lovingly delude
the aching brow that craves their tender care.

The wooing night: all nuptials are of her;
and she the musky golden cloud that hangs
on maiden blood that burns, a boding stir
shot thro' with flashes of alluring pangs,

far off, in creeks that slept unvisited
or moved so smoothly that no ripple creas'd
their mirror'd slip of blue, till that sweet dread
melted the air and soft sighs stole, releas'd;

and she the shame of brides, veiling the white
of bosoms that for sharp fulfilment yearn;
she is the obscure centre of delight
and steals the kiss, the kiss she would return

deepen'd with all the abysm that under speech
moves shudderingly, or as that gulf is known
to set the astonied spouses each from each
across the futile sea of sighs, alone.

All mystery, and all love, beyond our ken,
she woos us, mournful till we find her fair:
and gods and stars and songs and souls of men
are the sparse jewels in her scatter'd hair.

The Poor, Poor Country

JOHN SHAW NEILSON

Oh 'twas a poor county, in Autumn it was bare,
The only green was the cutting grass and the sheep found lit-
tle there.
Oh, the thin wheat and the brown oats were never two foot high,
But down in the poor country no pauper was I.

My wealth it was the glow that lives forever in the young,
'Twas on the brown water, in the green leaves it hung.
The blue cranes fed their young all day—how far in a tall tree!
And the poor, poor country made no pauper of me.

I waded out to the swan's nest—at night I heard them sing,
I stood amazed at the Pelican, and crowned him for a king;
I saw the black duck in the reeds, and the spoonbill on the sky,
And in that poor country no pauper was I.

The mountain-ducks down in the dark made many a hollow
sound,
I saw in sleep the Bunyip creep from the waters underground.
I found the plovers' island home, and they fought right
valiantly,
Poor was the country, but it made no pauper of me.

My riches all went into dreams that never yet came home,
They touched upon the wild cherries and the slabs of honey-
comb,

They were not of the desolate brood that men can sell or buy.
Down in that poor country no pauper was I.

*   *   *   *

The New Year came with heat and thirst and the little lakes
    were low,
The blue cranes were my nearest friends and I mourned to see
    them go;
I watched their wings so long until I only saw the sky,
Down in that poor country no pauper was I.

Elioth Gruner, Australia, 1882–1939, *Morning in the clearing*. Ballarat Fine Art Gallery.

The Diggers

LEON GELLERT

The diggers are digging, and digging deep.
They're digging and singing,
And I'm asleep.
They're digging and singing and swiftly they're swinging
The flying earth as it falls in a heap.
And some of it scatters and falls on my head,
But the diggers dig on. They can only dig.
They can only sing, and their eyes are big.
Their eyes are big and heavy as lead.
They dig and they sing and they think I'm dead.
The diggers are digging, and filling the hole.
They're sighing and sighing
They pray for my soul.

Frank Crozier, *The Beach at Anzac Cove, 25 April 1915.* Australian War Memorial.

I hear what they say, and from where I am lying,
I hear a new corporal calling the roll.
But the diggers dig on and fill in my bed.
The diggers dig on, and they sweat and they sweat.
They sigh and they sigh, and their eyes are wet.
The brown earth clatters and covers my head,
Then I laugh and I laugh, for they think I'm dead.

The Presence of the Bush

JOHN LE GAY BRERETON

In lonely gullies and secluded dells,
    And on the rocky hills and by the river,
I've whispered many a time
Soft secrets to the wind that never tells,
And many a fairy rhyme
    I've learnt where shade and light together quiver.

But all too weak am I to tell the tale
    The spirits of the sweet bush murmur to me;
I strive, but all in vain,
To sing the songs of wonderland—I fail
To give the notes again
    That like a wave of joy thrill through and through me.

The city has no pleasures like to these;
    In cramping walls the wind through crannies hisses
A curse of rankling hate,
But here it whispers love to all the trees,
And tinkling brooklets sate
    Their laughing souls in melodies of kisses.

Tom Roberts, Australia, 1856–1931, *Sherbrook Forest*, 1924, oil on canvas on paperboard 48 x 68.4 cm. Purchased 1946. Art Gallery of New South Wales.

And birds are here, and blossoms with a scent
   Of summer and the beauty of a dream;
But I am dazed, and though
My heart is full of music merged and blent
In streams of sound, I know
   The light I bring from them is but a gleam.

And I am lapped in glory, and I long
   For strength to share my joy with friend and foe;
Ah, friends! ah, brothers mine!
If I could blend my longings in a song,
   As grapes are crushed in wine,
You might hear words would make your spirits glow.

Break of Day

JOHN SHAW NEILSON

The stars are pale.
Old is the Night, his case is grievous,
His strength doth fail.

Through stilly hours
The dews have draped with Love's old lavishness
The drowsy flowers.

And Night shall die,
Already, lo! the Morn's first ecstasies
Across the sky.

An evil time is done.
Again, as some one lost in a quaint parable,
Comes up the Sun.

Walter Withers, Australia, 1854–1914, *Early Morning, Heidelberg*, 1898, oil on canvas on composition board 45 x 91.7 cm. Elder Bequest Fund 1899. Art Gallery of South Australia.

Another Fall of Rain

JOHN NEILSON

The weather had been sultry for a fortnight's time or more,
And the shearers had been driving might and main,
And some had got the century that never had before
But now all hands were wishing for the rain

Chorus
For the Boss is getting rusty and the ringer's caving in,
His bandaged wrist is aching with the pain,
And the second man, I fear, will make it hot for him
Unless we have another fall of rain.

A few had taken quarters and were coiling in their bunks
When we shore the six-tooth wethers from the plain.
And if the sheep get harder then a few more men will funk
Unless we get another fall of rain.

Chorus

But the sky is clouding over, and the thunder's muttering
loud,
And the clouds are driving eastward o'er the plain,
And I see the lightning flashing from the edge of yon black
cloud
And I hear the gentle patter of the rain.

Chorus

So lads, put on your stoppers, and let us to the hut.
We'll gather round and have a friendly game.
While some are playing music, and some play ante-up,
And some are gazing outward at the rain.

But now the rain is over, let the pressers spin the screw,
Let the teamsters back the wagons in again.
And we'll block the classer's table with the way we put them
    through,
For everything is merry since the rain.

Final chorus
And the Boss, he won't be rusty when his sheep they are all
    shorn,
And the ringer's wrist won't ache much with the pain
Of pocketing a season's cheque for fifty pounds or more,
And the second man will press him hard again.

Lambed Down

(Air—'Excelsior')
ANON.

The shades of night were falling fast,
As down a steep old gully passed
A man whom you could plainly see
Had just come off a drunken spree,
    Lambed down.

He'd left the station with his cheque,
And little evil did he reck;
At Ryan's pub he felt all right,
And yet he was, before the night,
    Lambed down.

Knocking down his cheque (engraving, after Samuel Calvert, from *Australasian Sketcher*,
18 November 1882). National Library of Australia.

"Oh, stay!" old Ryan said, "and slip
Your blanket off, and have a nip;
I'll cash your cheque and send you on."
He stopped and now his money's gone—
    Lambed down.

He's got the shakes and think he sees
Blue devils lurking in the trees;
Oh, shearers! if you've any sense
Don't be on any such pretence
    Lambed down.